SRA Art Connections

Artist Profiles

Level 1

SRA McGraw-Hill

Columbus, Ohio

A Division of The McGraw-Hill Companies

Cover: Agnes Tait. (American). *Skating in Central Park.* 1934. Oil on canvas. $33\frac{7}{8} \times 48\frac{1}{8}$ inches. National Museum of American Art, Smithsonian Institution, Washington, DC.

SRA/McGraw-Hill

A Division of The **McGraw·Hill** *Companies*

Send all inquiries to:
SRA/McGraw-Hill
250 Old Wilson Bridge Road
Suite 310
Worthington, OH 43085

Printed in the United States of America.

ISBN 0-02-688339-2

1 2 3 4 5 6 7 8 9 POH 01 00 99 98 97

Table of Contents

Thomas Hart Benton (tom´ əs härt bent´ ən)
(1889 – 1975)

About the Artist

Thomas Hart Benton was a regionalist American painter known for his energetic, colorful murals. He was the son of a United States congressman and named after his great uncle, the famous pre-American Civil War senator. From his family, Benton developed a strong identity as an American. Benton studied art at the Art Institute of Chicago and in Paris. He believed that American artists should develop their own styles and not simply copy French painting styles. Although Benton began his art career as a cartoonist, he was well-known for his murals depicting scenes from the rural past of the American South and Southwest.

ABOUT ART HISTORY

Benton painted subjects from mostly one region— the American Midwest. He helped develop and promote the American art style known as regionalism. He urged American artists to paint scenes from the lives of ordinary Americans. He also encouraged his students to try new ideas in their artwork. One of his students was the well-known painter Jackson Pollock.

ABOUT THE ARTWORK

Benton enjoyed painting Midwestern farm scenes. Many of his paintings show

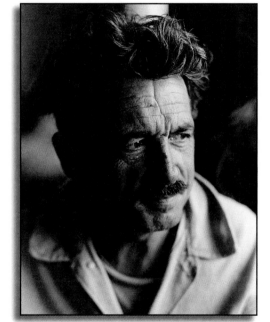

Corbis-Bettmann

sunburned farmers and huge work horses. In *Cradling Wheat,* several farmers and one of their sons are shown harvesting wheat by hand. Benton's paintings remind viewers of days gone by in rural America.

ABOUT THE MEDIA

Along with other media, Benton used oil and egg tempera.

ABOUT THE TECHNIQUE

Benton used his experience as a cartoonist in his later paintings. In some, he divided scenes with borders, like a comic strip.

Victor Brauner (vik´tər bron´ər)
(1903 – 1966)

About the Artist

Brauner was born in Romania and attended art school as a youth. He had his first exhibition in Bucharest in 1924 when he was only 21. He lived through World Wars I and II but did not take part in them. His friends included the surrealist painter Yves Tanguy and the surrealist writer André Breton. Both friends influenced his work. For the most part, Brauner was a thoughtful man who preferred to be alone. Like many surrealists, he also wrote poetry.

ABOUT ART HISTORY

Brauner's painting style became known as surrealism. Like other surrealists, Brauner wanted his art to disturb viewers. He wanted to shake up their way of seeing things. For example, in one painting, Brauner showed a glass hand holding a drinking glass made of skin. Surrealists tried to let their emotions and impulses direct their artwork.

Victor Brauner. (Rumanian). Prelude to a Civilization. *1954. Encaustic, and pen and ink, on Masonite. 51 × 79¾ inches. Metropolitan Museum of Art, New York, New York. The Jacques and Natasha Gelman Collection. Photograph by Malcolm Varon. © 1998 Artists Rights Society (ARS), New York/ADAGP, Paris.*

that time on, Brauner explored the world of magic and included symbols of magic in his paintings. Later, he created paintings that told myths.

In a poem, Brauner described his subject matter as an unknown dream world.

ABOUT THE ARTWORK

Early in his career, Brauner was fascinated with heads. He even painted men playing football using their own heads as balls. Then he became interested in eyes and often portrayed people with injured eyes. After painting these pictures, Brauner's left eye was injured when he tried to stop two friends from fighting. He lost his sight in that eye. Many people thought he had foreseen this accident and painted his own future. From

ABOUT THE MEDIA

Brauner made oil paintings and pencil drawings. He also created pictures with wax and with candle smoke.

ABOUT THE TECHNIQUE

Brauner sometimes made automatic drawings with his eyes closed. He wanted to let his unthinking impulses take over. He simply picked up a pencil and let it guide his drawing. He said, "I follow my hand, I understand gradually what I want to do. . . ."

Charles Burchfield (chärlz bûrch´fēld)
(1893 – 1967)

About the Artist

After high school, Charles Burchfield attended the Cleveland School of Art. He supported himself by working in industry. He served in the armed forces during World War I. After the war, he worked as a wallpaper designer. Burchfield began painting in 1915 and specialized in painting American small-town scenes and country life. In 1929, he was able to support himself as a full-time painter. After 1943, he concentrated on painting landscapes in watercolor. He was married and had five children.

Tom Hollyman

ABOUT ART HISTORY

Burchfield was one of the first American scene painters. His art style shifted from fantasy to realism and back to fantasy. In his early paintings, for example, buildings have faces. Later, he painted similar scenes but in a very realistic style. Still later, fantasy found its way back into his landscapes. He used symbols to represent emotions. A hooked spiral might mean fear. Burchfield based some of his last paintings on his earliest ones. He called these "reconstructions."

ABOUT THE ARTWORK

Many of Burchfield's landscapes are based on two cities where he lived: Salem, Ohio, and Buffalo, New York. Burchfield stressed the loneliness and dreariness he saw there. He also focused on the beauty in nature. He often had one lone tree as the center of a painting. Some of Burchfield's trees were realistic, and some were imaginary. His paintings show his deep interest in the weather and changing seasons.

ABOUT THE MEDIA

Burchfield worked in watercolors and sometimes in pencil.

ABOUT THE TECHNIQUE

Burchfield was interested in sounds and tried to symbolize them in his paintings. For example, he used wavy lines to show the hammering sound of a woodpecker. Small spots of black paint in some of his pictures represented musical notes. Burchfield used ideas from his earlier work as a wallpaper designer. He might fit sheets of paper together to make large paintings. This way, he could take out parts he didn't like and add new parts.

3

Nathaniel Bustion (nə than´ yəl būs tən)
(1942-   )

About the Artist

Nathaniel Bustion was born in Gadsen, Alabama, in 1942. He graduated from the Otis Art Institute, where he received a Master of Fine Arts degree. He also studied at the Belgium Antwerp Academy and attended several workshops at IFE University in Nigeria. Bustion's paintings, prints, and sculptures reflect his worldwide travels.

ABOUT ART HISTORY

Nathaniel Bustion is influenced by ancient African and Egyptian art. Many other artists have looked to cultures around the world for inspiration. Paul Gaugin moved from France to Tahiti so he could paint island imagery. A group of artists who called themselves symbolists followed his artistic examples. Gustave Moreau and Odilon Redon were two other symbolists. Pablo Picasso's cubist movement was inspired by African and Oceanic sculpture and masks.

Courtesy Nathaniel Bustion/ Mattinnii Studio

ABOUT THE ARTWORK

Bustion has created three series of artworks. His *Egyptian Mummies* is a bold series of symbolic prints showing Egyptian beliefs about the journey of the soul after death. The prints are geometric and abstract. The *African Masks* series focuses on African masks, faces, primitive patterns, and totems. Bustion's *Brownstone Series* is a collection of sculptures. They are long and tall like totem poles. On their surfaces, Bustion combines ancient African imagery and geometric designs with multiple faces. These faces often blend together into one headlike structure.

ABOUT THE MEDIA

Bustion's sculptures are made of stoneware, and some are cast in bronze. His clay sculptures are decorated with glossy and matte glazes. His prints are made of ink, paint, etching plates, and paper.

ABOUT THE TECHNIQUE

In his stoneware sculptures, Bustion builds forms by hand then shapes them with sculpture tools. He covers their surfaces with glazes in a variety of colors. He uses a casting process to make his bronze sculptures. His printmaking process is time-consuming and difficult. He uses a variety of printmaking processes to create his prints. He individualizes some of them using oil paints or airbrushing.

Mary Cassatt (mer´ē kə sat´)
(1844 – 1926)

About the Artist

Cassatt was born into a wealthy Pittsburgh family. She attended art school in Philadelphia. Eager to be on her own, she moved to Paris in 1866. She spent the rest of her life there. One of the many artists she met was the French Impressionist Degas, who painted her and influenced her painting style. By 1870, Cassatt was a successful artist. During her lifetime, her work was more popular in Europe than in the United States. Cassatt loved to entertain friends and ride her horses. As she got older, her eyesight began to fail. By 1914, she was unable to paint.

ABOUT ART HISTORY

Cassatt wanted to be known as an "artist," not a "woman artist." She was the only American artist included in the early shows of the French Impressionists. Cassatt urged many of her American friends to collect Impressionist paintings.

ABOUT THE ARTWORK

Cassatt is famous for painting mothers with their children, though she had no children of her own. Reportedly, Degas encouraged her to paint women and children.

Laura Platt Winfrey/
Woodfin Camp & Associates

At the time, few artists did so, except in religious scenes. Cassatt also painted quiet moments in the lives of women.

ABOUT THE MEDIA

Cassatt painted with oils. She made many pastel drawings and prints.

ABOUT THE TECHNIQUE

Cassatt mixed her colors directly on the canvas. Her compositions were strongly influenced by the asymmetrical arrangements of Japanese wood-block prints.

Marc Chagall (märk sha gäl´)
(1889 – 1985)

About the Artist

Chagall was born in Vitsyebsk, a small town in Russia, which is now part of Belarus. He studied art in Saint Petersburg and then in Paris. After the Russian revolution, he was the director of the Art Academy in his hometown. From 1919 to 1922, Chagall was the art director of the Art Academy in his hometown. From 1919 to 1922, Chagall was the art director of the Moscow Jewish State Theater. He painted murals in the theater lobby and created sets for the shows. In 1923, he moved to France, where he spent the rest of his life. except for a brief period of residence in the United States from 1941 to 1948.

ABOUT ART HISTORY

Chagall was one of the first people to paint pictures that looked like dreams. For example, he created many paintings of animals and people flying through the air, sometimes upside down. Chagall is sometimes called an early surrealist because of his dreamlike style and the element of fantasy in his work.

ABOUT THE ARTWORK

Chagall was born into a very religious Jewish family. His work shows the strong influence of his home and his heritage. He included childhood memories and religious images in his work. His works combine memories with folklore and fantasy. He created 12 stained glass windows in the Hadassah Hospital in Jerusalem, illustrating the Old Testament. He has created canvas

Sygma

murals for the ceiling of the Opera in Paris, in addition to two large canvas murals for the lobby of the new Metropolitan Opera House in New York City.

ABOUT THE MEDIA

This artist usually worked in oil paint on canvas. He also painted murals, created stained-glass windows, and designed costumes for ballet dancers.

ABOUT THE TECHNIQUE

Chagall remembered things from his childhood and drew them on the canvas. He covered the whole canvas with many pictures of different sizes. He sometimes drew people with just one big eye or animals that looked like monsters. He painted them in bright colors, such as red, blue, and yellow.

Helen Cordero (hel´ ən kôr dā´ rō)
(1916–   )

About the Artist

Helen Cordero began working with clay when she was 45 years old. Her children were grown and she was looking for a way to make a little extra money. Her bowls and jars kept coming out crooked. She was ready to quit when a friend suggested that she try making figures instead. She started to make frogs, birds, and eventually little people.

The first time she showed her figures, a folk art collector bought all her pieces and commissioned her to do a 250-piece nativity scene. Thinking of her *Singing Mother* piece, he also asked her to make a larger seated figure with children. Cordero said she thought about her grandfather who was always surrounded by children as he told stories. Remembering her grandfather's voice, she shaped her first *Storyteller Doll* in 1964, beginning a new tradition.

ABOUT ART HISTORY
Cordero revived an almost eradicated tradition of figurative pottery. When she shaped the first *Storyteller Doll* in 1964, she reinvented a Cochiti tradition of figurative pottery. Today, hundreds of potters are producing storyteller dolls. Some are animals such as a storyteller bear covered with little cubs, and an owl singing to owlets.

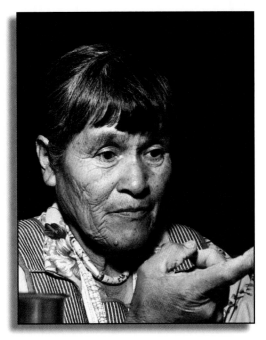

Copyright © 1996, The Heard Museum (Phoenix, AZ)/Photo by Al Abrams

ABOUT THE ARTWORK
Cordero's *Storyteller Dolls* are usually seated with their eyes closed and their mouths open, as if they are singing or telling stories. Each of her figures is different. She never makes an exact duplicate.

ABOUT THE MEDIA
Cordero makes her figures from the red clay that is gathered on or near the reservation.

She covers them with several coats of white slip. Then, red and black details are added. The black paint, or *guaco*, is made by boiling wild spinach (Rocky Mountain Bee Plant) into a sludge. This sludge hardens into a cake that is used like watercolor paint.

ABOUT THE TECHNIQUE
Cordero shapes each figure and lets it dry. Then she sands it smooth and coats it with a thin wash of gray clay and water. Cordero fires her figures on a grate in her yard. She applies more wash and fires the figures again, until she achieves the color she wants. Finally, she paints on the faces, hair, and costumes.

Leonardo da Vinci (lā ō när´ dō dä vin´ chē)
(1452 – 1519)

About the Artist

Leonardo was born on April 15, 1452, in a small Tuscan town of Vinci. He was the son of a wealthy Florentine notary and a peasant woman. Even as a child, people saw that he had remarkable abilities. He had gracious manners, a fine sense of humor, great strength, and a curiosity that drove him to explore everything. In the mid-1460s, the family settled in Florence, where Leonardo was given the best education in art and other intellectual pursuits. He was apprenticed to Verrocchio as a studio boy in 1466. By 1478, he was listed as an independent master painter.

Leonardo was a genius and showed great skill at everything he tried. As he grew older, he studied architecture, mathematics, sculpture, painting, anatomy, poetry, literature, music, geology, botany, and hydraulics. He completed over 120 notebooks full of drawings and written observations. He wrote everything in a mirror writing, a way of writing backwards that could be read by viewing the reflection in a mirror.

ABOUT ART HISTORY
Leonardo's work is considered the high point of Renaissance art. Leonardo was a genius whose achievements spread into many fields. The young Leonardo wrote, "It is easy to become a universal man," and so he did. He was an engineer, architect, inventor, physician, musician, and astronomer. Today, his designs for the helicopter, tank, and other inventions have been built and powered by modern engineers.

ABOUT THE ARTWORK
One of Leonardo's most famous works is the *Mona Lisa*, which he carried with him

Self-Portrait

on trips. Another is the *Last Supper;* which took him three years to complete.

ABOUT THE MEDIA
Leonardo painted in oils, tempera, and a mixture of the two. Some of his experimental paint combinations caused his artwork to flake away. He also worked in sculpture and designed costumes and play settings.

ABOUT THE TECHNIQUE
This artist used shadows to make his subjects look three-dimensional. He blurred backgrounds and created aerial perspective.

Stuart Davis (stū´ ərt dā´ vəs)
(1894 – 1964)

About the Artist

Davis was born in Philadelphia. He left high school when he was only 16 years old to go to New York to study art. His long career began when he showed some paintings in the Armory Show in New York City in 1913. This large and important show introduced modern art to many Americans. Afterwards, Stuart's career took off. By the 1920s, Davis was studying cubism. Through the 1940s, many of his paintings showed his love of jazz music. He even gave some of his paintings musical titles.

ABOUT ART HISTORY
Cubism is a style of art first developed by Pablo Picasso of Spain and George Braque of France in the early 1900s. The cubists simplified forms into their basic geometric shapes. This style influenced Davis, and he, too, simplified objects into flat-looking, colored shapes.

ABOUT THE ARTWORK
Davis was interested in city scenes with many people and factories. He painted pictures of streets in Manhattan and Paris using colorful, geometric shapes. He also painted dense canvases full of many abstract forms. Sometimes he reworked the same picture

© 1957 Arnold Newman

several times to explore different ways of arranging and coloring the shapes. Often his own unusual signature is part of the composition.

ABOUT THE MEDIA
This artist generally worked in oil paint on canvas.

ABOUT THE TECHNIQUE
Davis began by making many drawings of what he was going to paint. Each time, he simplified the shape. After drawing the shapes exactly on the canvas, he painted them in bright, solid colors.

Albrecht Dürer (äl brekt dū ər)
(1471–1528)

About the Artist

Dürer was born in Nuremberg, Germany in 1471, the second son in a family of eighteen children. His father was a goldsmith and it was assumed that he would follow in the family tradition. Since Dürer displayed such skill in drawing, his father apprenticed him to a local painter when he was 15. He married and traveled to Italy when he was 23. In Italy, he was introudced to the Renaissance ideal of the artist as intellectual. He brought this philosophy back to Nuremberg, and set about educating himself in all fields of learning associated with this new approach to art. He studied and wrote about geometry, perspective, proportion, and the nature of art. He also wrote many letters and kept a diary. He was observant, imaginative, energetic, and popular. Many political and religious leaders of this turbulent period were Dürer's friends.

ABOUT ART HISTORY

Dürer was the most famous artist of Reformation Germany. He was known for his paintings, drawings, prints, and theoretical writings on art. He incorporated the art of Renaissance Italy into the Gothic traditions of his country. He had a strong influence on his contemporaries.

ABOUT THE ARTWORK

Like other artists of his time, Dürer painted many religious scenes. He often placed small animals in his paintings. For example, his *Adam and Eve* included a cat, an elk, a rabbit, an ox, and other animals. His images of animals and nature were so detailed and realistic that they could have been used in textbooks. Dürer also excelled at portrait

Self-Portrait. *Museo del Prado, Madrid, Spain/Scala/Art Resource, NY.*

painting and painted himself many times. He had a technical mastery of printmaking.

ABOUT THE MEDIA

Dürer painted with watercolors on paper, and he used oil on wood and canvas backing. He made many drawings using charcoal and chalk, and produced prints done with engraving and woodcut techniques.

ABOUT THE TECHNIQUE

Dürer's training as an engraver and designer of woodcuts gave him excellent drawing skills. His portraits show the heart and soul of the person as well as an accurate likeness. He painted so smoothly that you cannot see any brush strokes.

About the Artist

Fonseca was born in California. He has Native American (Maidu), Portuguese, and Hawaiian ancestors. After studying art and Native American myths in college, Fonseca began to listen closely to the stories told by his elderly relatives. He decided to use his art skills to help preserve his culture. At first, he worked as a janitor and business manager of a reservation so that he could buy painting supplies. In 1977, he finished his first major work, *The Creation Story*. It tells the history of the Maidu people. Then Fonseca decided to paint Coyote, a trickster character who represents both good and bad in Native American stories. He first painted Coyote in Native American clothing. But soon Fonseca dressed Coyote in jeans, high-top tennis shoes, and a black jacket.

ABOUT ART HISTORY

Fonseca has helped place Native American art in a contemporary setting. He uses humor to help people see their weaknesses, especially their disrespect for other cultures. He says, "When one is happy, it is easier to accept and learn new things."

ABOUT THE ARTWORK

Fonseca's best-known paintings are the Coyote series. Through Coyote, Fonseca pokes fun at people, including tourists who buy Native American handiwork. *Snapshot or Wish You Were Here, Coyote,* for example, shows coyote "tourists" wearing Hawaiian shirts and posing in front of Native American pueblos. Fonseca painted Coyote and his girlfriend

Harry Fonseca in his Santa Fe studio with recent works. Photo by Yvonne Bond. Courtesy of the Wheelwright Museum

Rose as ballet stars. More recently, Fonseca has created a series called *Stone Poems*. These paintings are based on petroglyphs on rocks in the Mojave Desert. The series combines ancient drawings and modern art.

ABOUT THE MEDIA

This artist works in oils, silkscreen, watercolors, ink, lithograph, collage, and other media.

ABOUT THE TECHNIQUE

Fonseca describes his art as flat and direct, but he loves to experiment. For example, he once glued a red velvet "curtain" to a painting of Coyote as a ballet dancer. He also added glitter to a picture to make Coyote sparkle.

Carmen Lomas Garza

(kär´ mān lō´ mäs gär´ sä) *(1948 –   )*

About the Artist

Lomas Garza was born in Kingsville, Texas. She grew up in a Hispanic home where both Spanish and English were spoken. When she and her brother started school, many of their classmates made fun of them for speaking English with an accent. Lomas Garza often felt that she did not fit in at school. This feeling led her to develop stronger ties with her family and community. She decided she wanted to be an artist when she was only 13 years old. She studied art at the Texas Arts and Industry University and earned her master's degree from San Francisco State University.

Hulleah Tsinhnahjinnie

ABOUT ART HISTORY

Lomas Garza is a major contemporary Hispanic artist. Her aim is to produce works of art that show the beauty of Hispanic culture.

ABOUT THE ARTWORK

Lomas Garza's paintings tell stories about growing up as a Hispanic in Texas. She paints many *monitos,* or little people paintings. These paintings often portray families taking part in such everyday activities as dancing, working, preparing food, or eating.

ABOUT THE MEDIA

This artist paints mainly with oil, acrylic, or gouache paint on canvas or linen. She also makes etchings, paper cutouts, and prints.

ABOUT THE TECHNIQUE

Lomas Garza often uses rich colors and simple shapes in her paintings.

Ellen Day Hale (el´ ən dā hāl)
(1855-1940)

About the Artist

Hale was born in Boston. She was part of a prominent, talented family. Her great-uncle was Nathan Hale, the patriot. Harriet Beecher Stowe, who wrote *Uncle Tom's Cabin,* and Catherine Beecher, who fought for women's rights, were her great-aunts. Ellen's father served as chaplain of the United States Senate. He was also a photographer and the author of *Man Without a Country.* Artist Susan Hale, Ellen's aunt, gave her lessons in watercolor. One of Ellen's seven brothers, Philip Leslie Hale, also became an artist.

After studying art, Ellen opened her own studio in 1877 and began teaching art. Later she studied drawing and etching in Paris. She developed her own style and began receiving requests for portraits and church decorations. Hale traveled extensively and served as her father's hostess for the two years that he was the Senate chaplain. She spent her summers on the Massachusetts coast where she etched the landscape. Hale, who also wrote poetry and a book titled *History of Art,* was an unusual woman for the nineteenth century, independent and free-spirited.

ABOUT ART HISTORY
Hale's Impressionist style was influenced by a number of artists, some of whom were her teachers. They included William Morris Hunt, Helen Knowlton, William Rimmer, Gabrielle Clements (who taught her etching), René Ligeron, James Whistler, and the French Impressionists.

ABOUT THE ARTWORK
Hale's artwork included scenes of everyday life, still lifes, landscapes, and altarpieces. She often focused on women busy with tasks at home. For example,

Sophia Smith Collection, Smith College

in the work titled *June,* she painted a woman sewing.

ABOUT THE MEDIA
Besides oil paintings and watercolors, Hale was skilled in etching, including drypoint, and aquatint.

ABOUT THE TECHNIQUE
This artist first painted in the broad, bold style she learned from William Morris Hunt. Later, as she used lighter colors and stronger highlights, her pictures became Impressionist "portraits of light."

Lawren S. Harris (lôr´ ən hâr´ is)
(1885 – 1970)

About the Artist

Harris was a Canadian from a wealthy family. He was in college when a math professor noticed his pencil drawings. The professor talked Harris's mother into sending him to art school. After studying art in Germany, Harris began his career by illustrating magazine articles. In 1908, on a trip for a magazine, Harris saw his first winter in the Canadian wilderness. He showed that winter beauty in his realistic art. By the time Harris married in 1910, he was already selling his paintings. In 1930, he took a dangerous two-month cruise on a Canadian supply ship into the frozen Arctic. Afterward he painted many scenes from that vast wilderness. After a divorce and remarriage, Harris shifted to abstract art. Then he created his favorite winter landscapes with triangles and spheres.

ABOUT ART HISTORY
Harris and six other Canadian painters formed an artists organization called the Group of Seven. The painters helped promote their nation's artists. Harris liked to try new styles and paint different things.
He is known as a regionalist painter. He is one of Canada's most important artists.

ABOUT THE ARTWORK
Harris loved winter landscapes. He especially loved the beauty of snow-topped fir trees. His paintings often showed the northern lights on fields of snow and ice. He also drew poor urban neighborhoods, but he seemed more interested in the buildings than in the people who lived there.

McMichael Canadian Art Collection Archives.
Photo by Robert McMichael.

ABOUT THE MEDIA
Harris used pencil, charcoal, watercolors, and oils.

ABOUT THE TECHNIQUE
This artist most often used soft, muted colors, such as mauve, pink, pale blue, and cream. Many of his urban scenes included strong horizontal and vertical lines that gave structure to the paintings. In landscapes, his strong brush strokes show the rugged land.

Hans Hofmann (hänz hof′män)
(1880 – 1966)

About the Artist

This German painter studied art in his homeland and in Paris before opening his own school in Munich, Germany. In 1915, Hans Hofmann opened a school of modern art in Munich, Germany. As World War II threatened, some of his students who had already moved to New York City arranged a teaching position for him at the Art Students League. Hofmann emigrated to the United States and settled in New York City in 1932. In 1933, he started the Hans Hofmann School of Fine Art. It became one of the most respected art schools in the United States. For the next thirty years, Hofmann taught art but did little painting of his own. In 1958, he left his school to paint full time. He eventually achieved international recognition.

ABOUT ART HISTORY

Hofmann's early paintings were expressionist landscapes and still lifes. He strongly admired the work of the Russian abstract painter Wassily Kandinsky. In time, Hofmann's work became totally non-objective. He led the way for painters in the United States to move into abstract expressionism. He was called the dean of abstract expressionism because he influenced so many New York artists. Hofmann also contributed greatly to modern art by focusing on the psychological effects of color and other elements of painting.

ABOUT THE ARTWORK

Like other abstract expressionist painters, Hofmann shared his feelings and ideas in

Courtesy Andre Emmerich Gallery

purely abstract images. He used combinations of red, yellow, and green, for example, to express what he called "push-pull tension." The reds and yellows push forward, while the greens pull back from the viewer.

ABOUT THE MEDIA

Hofmann worked mainly in oils.

ABOUT THE TECHNIQUE

This artist used brilliant colors, lines that seemed to be moving, and thick layers of paint. In his painting *Flowering Swamp,* for example, two rectangles seem to float over thick layers of color. The combination suggests flowers floating on water.

Winslow Homer (winz´ lō hō´ mər)
(1836 – 1910)

About the Artist

Homer was born in Boston. He had very little formal training in art. But he showed his great artistic talent even in his earliest sketches. He worked as a magazine illustrator for nearly twenty years. When the Civil War began, *Harper's Weekly* sent him to the front lines to sketch both the fighting and the everyday life. Homer did not begin to paint seriously until he was 26. He taught himself the techniques he needed. He eventually settled on the Maine coast. In his later years, Homer lived like a hermit, seldom seeing anyone.

ABOUT ART HISTORY

Homer avoided other artists, other art styles, and art exhibits. He once said, "If one wishes to become a real artist, one must never look at the work of another artist." His first paintings were very detailed. His later work was simpler and more creative. Homer led American art out of the romanticism of the mid-1800s and into the peak of realism.

ABOUT THE ARTWORK

Homer loved nature, especially the sea. Even when he lived in New York City, he never painted city scenes. He painted scenes from nature. Over the years, he changed from painting families in farm scenes to painting men struggling with nature, usually the sea. During this period, he painted *The Fog Warning*. It shows a man alone in a small

Culver Pictures

boat on a rough sea. Toward the end of his life, Homer stopped putting people into his paintings. Instead, he focused only on nature.

ABOUT THE MEDIA

Homer is best known for his watercolors. He also created sketches, wood engravings, and oil paintings. In addition, he worked in charcoal, chalk, and pencil.

ABOUT THE TECHNIQUE

Homer was very patient and particular about details. For example, he waited for months for the light to be just right when he was painting *Early Morning at Sea*. He also used watercolors in an unusual way for his time. Instead of coloring in light areas with white paint, he left the paper white.

Wolf Kahn (wulf kän)
(1927 –)

About the Artist

Kahn was born in Germany to Jewish parents. His mother died when he was five. He lived in Germany with his grandmother for a while. Then, he was sent to England in 1939, just before World War II broke out. The next year he traveled to the United States to live with his father. As a young man, Kahn studied abstract expressionist painting. Now he has his own approach to art. In the early 1950s, Kahn helped set up an art gallery in New York City. Since then, his work has been shown nationwide.

Walter Weisman/Globe Photos

ABOUT ART HISTORY

Kahn is sometimes called "a school of one." He mixes realism with abstraction to show a style called abstract expressionism. Rather than show exactly what he sees, he shows how a scene makes him feel. He uses layers of color and light. Kahn's work is also called "modernist."

ABOUT THE ARTWORK

In his work, Kahn tries to show the shifting light and atmosphere in landscapes. He is interested in the natural difference between sky and land. The sky is very light, but the land is heavy. Kahn often uses more color in the sky and less color in the land.

ABOUT THE MEDIA

Kahn works in pastels, which he calls "the dust on the butterflies' wings." Pastels are sticks of colored powder mixed with oils; they are similar to chalk. Kahn likes pastels because they can show sharp contrasts and delicate tints. He believes that the dusty quality of the powder adds to the beauty of his pictures.

ABOUT THE TECHNIQUE

Kahn uses glowing violets, oranges, and pinks, along with quiet grays. These give Kahn the hazy images he likes. He adds layers of colors until he gets the effect he wants. Kahn often creates a quick sketch outdoors and then completes it in his studio. He might also paint the same scene in larger or smaller versions.

Ellsworth Kelly (elz´ wûrth kel´ ē)
(1923-   )

About the Artist

Kelly was born in Newburgh, New York. He had two brothers. During high school, he studied art and theater. For a while, he could not decide which he wanted as a career. He eventually chose art. In 1941, he began to study at the Pratt Institute in Brooklyn, New York. In 1943, he volunteered to serve in the army during World War II. After the war, he went back to his art studies. He studied at the School of the Museum of Fine Arts in Boston, Massachusetts. From 1948 to 1954, he lived in France, studying art and architecture. In 1954, he returned to New York.

ABOUT ART HISTORY

Kelly was a leader of the hard-edge Color-Field painting artistic movement. Color-Field painting began during the late 1950s. In this style of painting, the canvas is stained with thin and translucent color washes. The color washes are made of acrylic, ink, or oil that can be diluted. Mixed with a solvent, the color flows freely.

ABOUT THE ARTWORK

Kelly created sculptures influenced by the Color-Field painting movement. He used the same geometric shapes and colors of this painting style. He used painting canvases for his early sculptures. His best-known later works are his panel paintings, which consist of several canvases, as many as 64, joined together. Each canvas is painted a different, intense color.

Dan Budnik/Woodfin Camp & Associates

ABOUT THE MEDIA

Kelly integrated painting and sculpture. He experimented with the shapes and sizes of canvases. These experiments led him to explore sculpture and three-dimensional or free-standing art. He was very interested in color and shape.

ABOUT THE TECHNIQUE

Kelly wanted his works to communicate unexpected effects. He paid great attention to details of color and shape in his work. He created unexpected effects by changing these details. His paintings were often only one color or black and white. The canvases were different shapes. Placing one painting next to other paintings of similar size but different colors created an unexpected effect. In his sculpture, Kelly experimented with the different shapes of objects and how the shapes related to each other.

About the Artist

Lawrence's parents met on their migration to the North. Lawrence was born in Atlantic City in 1917. The family finally settled in Harlem in 1929, at the end of the Harlem Renaissance. Because his mother worked all day, she enrolled Jacob in the Harlem Art Workshop after school to keep him out of trouble. He had many excellent teachers, including Charles Alston. Lawrence won a scholarship to the American Artists school. During World War II he served in the Coast Guard and painted a series of paintings about his experiences. They were exhibited by the Museum of Modern Art in 1944. He taught at New York's Pratt Institute from 1958 to 1965. From 1970, he taught at the University of Washington in Seattle where he also served as head of the art department. He retired in 1983.

ABOUT ART HISTORY

Lawrence's paintings not only contribute to the art world, but they also add to our knowledge of African American history.

ABOUT THE ARTWORK

Lawrence's most famous work is a series of 60 paintings called *The Migration of the Negro*. The paintings tell the story of the migration, starting at a train station in the South and ending at a station in the North. The scenes he chose to paint focus on the struggle of leaving one life for another and the search for freedom and dignity. His paintings did not overlook the harshness and violence that was part of this migration. Lawrence has also

Black Images

painted African American heroes, such as Harriet Tubman and Frederick Douglass.

ABOUT THE MEDIA

Lawrence paints on paper with gouache (gwäsh). This is an opaque watercolor paint, similar to the tempera paint used in schools. It covers the paper with a smooth, matte coat. He is also a printmaker.

ABOUT THE TECHNIQUE

Lawrence says a lot about his subjects with only a few lines and carefully chosen colors. He tends to use many neutral colors, such as taupe, mocha, and charcoal. He balances them with splashes of bright color.

Roy Lichtenstein (roi lik´tən stīn)
(1923 –   )

About the Artist

After earning a degree in art and teaching at several colleges, Roy Lichtenstein is a recognized pop art painter, graphic artist, and sculptor. This American artist is best known for his large-scale interpretations of comic-strip art. Lichtenstein continues to experiment with colors, shapes, media, and subjects.

ABOUT ART HISTORY

Lichtenstein helped introduce pop art in the early 1960s. His goal was to help people see everyday objects in new ways. Pop artists choose subjects from the popular culture, so their work is called Pop Art. His early work was in the abstract expressionist style, but after 1957 he began to experiment with cartoon images from bubble gum wrappers.

Photo © Timothy Greenfield-Sanders

ABOUT THE ARTWORK

This artist often creates a series of paintings on a theme, such as rooms in a house. He is well known for his drawings of comic-strip characters, and he often includes dialogue in balloons above their heads. He also has done several paintings and sculptures of brush strokes. In the majority of his works, Lichtenstein imitates and enlarges Ben-day dots. His later works include interpretations of romance characters and stylized landscapes, showing the influence of Matisse and Picasso.

ABOUT THE MEDIA

Lichtenstein's work includes oil and acrylic paintings, silkscreens, woodcuts, and bronze sculptures. Sometimes he experiments with other media, such as India ink on acetate.

ABOUT THE TECHNIQUE

Lichtenstein begins by sketching a small version of his idea on paper. He uses lots of dots and diagonal lines.

He then projects an image of the sketch onto a stretched canvas. Tracing the projected pattern, he draws the design on the canvas. Sometimes he adds black tape to mark the lines he will paint, or he may use large circle templates for dots.

Lastly, he paints in the colored areas and the black lines. Lichtenstein chooses flat, primary colors and uses several coats so that his brush strokes won't show. Masking tape, templates, rulers, and other tools help keep his lines straight and neat.

Henri Matisse (än rē´ mä tēs´)
(1869 – 1954)

About the Artist

Henri Matisse was the son of a middle-class couple in the north of France. He was not interested in art while he was in school. After high school, his father sent him to law school in Paris. When he was 21, an appendicitis attack changed his life. Because he had to spend a long time in the hospital, his mother brought him a paint box to help him pass the time. Matisse eventually convinced his father to let him drop out of law school and study art.

Matisse married and soon had a family. His paintings weren't selling, so he worked for a decorator and his wife opened a hat shop. During his last years of life, he sufferd from arthritis. Unable to hold a brush in his hands, he devoted his efforts to making paper cutouts from papers painted to his specifications and created fantastic, brightly colored shapes. Unlike many other artists, he was internationally famous during his lifetime.

ABOUT ART HISTORY
In 1905, Matisse exhibited with his friends in a painting style showing strong emotionalism, wild colors, and distortion of shape. They were called *les fauves,* or the wild beasts. They experimented with intense, sometimes violent colors. Without letting their work become abstract, Matisse and other Fauve painters tested the bounds of reality.

ABOUT THE ARTWORK
Matisse painted still lifes, room interiors, and landscapes. His paintings of dancers and human figures were generally more concerned with expressive shape than accurate representation of anatomy.

UPI/Corbis-Bettmann

At one time, he was asked to design a chapel. He designed the entire structure, including the stained glass windows and the vestments for the priests.

ABOUT THE MEDIA
Matisse painted primarily with oils. He created many prints. Later in life, he worked with cut paper.

ABOUT THE TECHNIQUE
Matisse worked with bold, intense colors. He simplified and distorted shapes for expressive qualities. He was more interested in the way the visual elements were organized than in realistic representation.

About the Artist

McKelvey, a Navajo, grew up in the mountains of New Mexico. Her family got its water from the streams and a well near their home. As a child, McKelvey went to the well with her friends and siblings to get water. The children played in the clay near the well. McKelvey learned at an early age that wet clay could be shaped into interesting forms. She took a pottery class in college as part of her training to become an elementary school teacher. Later, she taught herself how to make pots.

ABOUT ART HISTORY

McKelvey is a Navajo folk artist. Her pottery, which is both useful and beautiful, reflects her Navajo culture.

ABOUT THE ARTWORK

McKelvey creates pots that show the influence of the Southwest, where she has spent her entire life. Her pots are covered with striking designs of Navajo origin.

Courtesy of Lucy Leuppe McKelvey

ABOUT THE TECHNIQUE

McKelvey creates pots using the coil method of construction, which is the oldest and simplest method. After preparing the clay, she shapes part of it into a flat piece for the base of the pot. The remaining clay is rolled into long strips. Using the base piece as a foundation, McKelvey coils the strips of clay on top of one another. Each coil layer is attached to the next with slip, a combination of water and clay. McKelvey always smooths the inside surface of her pottery. Sometimes she also smooths the outside surface, depending on the design of the piece. She decorates the outside surface using sharp tools and brushes. The pottery is fired in an oven called a kiln.

ABOUT THE MEDIA

The distinctive terra-cotta, or brownish orange, coloring of her pottery comes from the dry climate of the Southwest interacting with the clay. Other colors in her pottery come from the herbs and plants in the region.

Piet Mondrian (pēt mon´drē än)
(1872–1944)

About the Artist

Mondrian's name was Pieter Cornelis Mondrian, but he liked to be called Piet Mondrian. He was born in the Netherlands. Mondrian's family was Calvinist. At a young age, Mondrian could not decide between studying religion or art. He finally decided he wanted to be a painter. However, his parents wanted him to be a teacher. He studied to be a teacher and later studied art for three years at the Amsterdam Academy. Mondrian then attended evening art classes and worked during the day painting portraits, paintings of people, and copies of older paintings at museums in Amsterdam. During his life, Mondrian traveled around Europe and lived in many places.

Mondrian was one of the most influential twentieth century artists. His theories altered the course of painting and had a profound influence on architecture, industrial design, and graphic arts. He moved to New York City in 1940 to escape the war, and he died there in 1944.

ABOUT ART HISTORY

Mondrian carried abstraction to its furthest limits. He sought to expose the basic principles that underlie all visual images. Along with Theo van Doesburg, he founded a magazine named *De Stijl.* In it, he explained his theories of a new art form he called neoplasticism. He said art should express only the universal absolutes that underlie reality.

ABOUT THE ARTWORK

Mondrian painted in many different styles. As a young artist, he sat on riverbanks and painted landscapes. After a visit to Spain, his style changed. He began to order and repeat objects and experiment with color in his paintings. He rejected all

Laurie Platt Winfrey/Woodfin Camp & Associates

sensuous qualities of textures, surface, and color, reducing his palette to flat, primary colors. When he moved to New York City in 1940, his style became freer and more rhythmic, such as in *Broadway Boogie-Woogie,* which he painted in 1942.

ABOUT THE TECHNIQUE

Mondrian wanted to create balance in his paintings. He was interested in relationships among different colors, lines, and shapes. He did not use many colors in his paintings. He generally painted with the primary colors of blue, red, and yellow and the neutral colors of black and white. He depended on his feelings to tell him when a work was finished.

Claes Oldenburg (kläs ōl´ dən bərg)
(1929 –)

About the Artist

Born in Sweden, Oldenburg became a United States citizen in 1953. He studied writing at Yale and art at the Art Institute of Chicago. When he moved to New York City in 1956, he felt an urge to sculpt the city, so he created *The Store*. This was a painted sculpture of clothes and food displayed as if they were in a New York shop window. In 1961, Oldenburg opened a real store in New York City and stocked it with plaster food for sale. The next year he created "happenings"—mixtures of sound, movement, people, and giant cloth objects stuffed with rags or paper. This led to his first well-known art form: soft sculpture. Recently, Oldenburg has created metal sculptures of everyday objects, greatly enlarged. Examples of his enormous sculptures include a typewriter eraser, 7 feet tall, and a teaspoon, 29 feet long.

ABOUT ART HISTORY

Oldenburg was a leader of the Pop Art movement in the 1960s. He wanted art to celebrate life and to make people more aware of everyday objects. He wrote, "I am for an art that takes its lines from life itself, that twists and extends and accumulates and spits and drips, and is heavy and coarse and blunt and sweet and stupid as life itself." Sometimes he exaggerates the characteristics of an everyday object, changing it into an abstract form.

Timothy Greenfield-Sanders

For example, he built a 45-foot-tall steel clothespin in Centre Square in Philadelphia. He often makes soft, collapsing sculptures of hard items such as typewriters, toilets, and drum sets to draw attention to the form of the real items.

ABOUT THE MEDIA

Besides soft and hard sculpture, Oldenburg creates drawings, watercolors, and prints of the subjects of his sculpture.

ABOUT THE ARTWORK

Oldenburg is famous for his giant sculptures that he creates from steel or from soft materials like stuffed canvas. He sculpts ice-cream cones, electric plugs, hamburgers, lipstick tubes, and other everyday items.

ABOUT THE TECHNIQUE

This artist draws his subjects before sculpting them. His soft sculptures are cut from canvas, sewn, stuffed with foam rubber, and painted. His large metal pieces are constructed in foundries devoted to creating sculpture from his models and work under his supervision.

Mark Rothko (märk roth´ kō)
(1903–1970)

About the Artist

Mark Rothko was born in Russia. His birth name was Marcus Rothkovich. His family moved to the United States when he was only ten years old. They settled in Portland, Oregon. Rothko attended Yale University between 1921 and 1923. He also spent some time studying at the Art Student's League in New York City, but was largely a self-taught artist.

For several years after his death, his estate was the subject of bitter legal battles. His executors sold his work at prices that cheated his heirs. His daughter staged a daring rescue of his paintings at the New York City docks just minutes before they were to be shipped out of the country and out of her reach.

© Dan Budnik/Woodfin Camp & Associates, Inc.

ABOUT ART HISTORY

Rothko was one of the pioneers of the abstract expressionist movement of the 1950s. He was also associated with the New York School painters. These were a group of post-World War II artists who created raw, powerful, and original paintings. His work belongs to the Color-Field branch of abstract expressionism.

ABOUT THE ARTWORK

Rothko began his career as a social realist. He painted recognizable subjects such as city scenes, plants, and animals. Gradually his work became nonobjective. He created large rectangles of color with blurry edges. He used color to control the emotional impact of his shapes.

ABOUT THE MEDIA

Rothko worked mainly with oil on canvas.

ABOUT THE TECHNIQUE

Mark Rothko believed that his works of art were living things. One way that he attempted to bring life to the shapes that he created was through a style of freehand painting and drawing known as automatism. Automatism allows the creative side of the brain to overtake the artwork. Rothko simply let his hand draw freely. He felt that this allowed him more freedom of expression.

Miriam Schapiro (mîr´ ē əm shə pîr´ ō)
(1923-)

About the Artist

Miriam Schapiro is an American artist who was born in Toronto, Canada. She grew up in the Flatbush section of Brooklyn, New York. Her parents encouraged her interests in art and sent her to art classes at the Museum of Modern Art.

She met her husband, Paul Brach, while attending college. They married in 1946 and have a son who is a writer. Schapiro organizes her home life so that art is woven into it. She can move from baking in the kitchen to painting in her studio and back to the kitchen without feeling interrupted. Her husband says that she has learned to live a "seamless life."

ABOUT ART HISTORY

In the beginning of Schapiro's career, her work was abstract expressionist, action art. Later, she became an important leader in the feminist art movement of the early 1970s. She wished to have art speak as a woman speaks. In art history, women's art has been hidden. Even the materials that women have used–lace, fabric, tea towels, ribbon, sequins, buttons, rickrack, yarn, silk, cotton, and so on–have been left out of art history.

*© Suzanne Opton/
Courtesy Steinbaum Krauss Gallery*

Schapiro and Sherry Brody made "The Dollhouse"–a construction of bits of fabric and tiny household objects meant to reflect female life and fantasy. Schapiro also made "femmages." She and a few other artists invented this word to describe art made with techniques that women traditionally use. Examples are sewing, embroidery, piece work, and appliqué. Femmages are collages reflecting female emotions and creativity.

ABOUT THE ARTWORK

Schapiro's first works were abstract expressionism. In time, her work became more geometrical and structured. In the 1950s, her work expressed female identity in a man's world. She began to include feminist themes in her art. In 1972, Schapiro and other female artists changed an old Hollywood mansion into a totally female environment and called it "womanhouse."

ABOUT THE MEDIA

Schapiro used fabric scraps, sequins, buttons, threads, rickrack, spangles, yarn, silk, taffeta, cotton, burlap, wool, and other materials that a woman might use in daily life.

ABOUT THE TECHNIQUE

Schapiro uses collage, assemblage, and decoupage to put materials together.

Kurt Schwitters (kûrt shvit´ərs)
(1887–1948)

About the Artist

Kurt Schwitters was born in Hannover, Germany, in 1887. He went to art school there, and he also learned to write poetry. He created a magazine in 1923. Schwitters began painting as an expressionist, but he turned to collage in 1919. He lived in Sweden for a while and then in London, England, where he died when he was 61. Many artists have been influenced by his ideas in their own work.

Karger-Decker/Interfoto

ABOUT ART HISTORY

Schwitters made works of art in a strange style called Dada. (The word *Dada* was chosen mainly because the artists wanted a meaningless word to represent their movement.) Dadaists made art by combining unrelated objects. They wanted to create art that looked like it was put together by chance or luck. After 1922, his work became more carefully organized, influenced by the Dutch group known as *De Stijl*.

ABOUT THE ARTWORK

This artist created a special kind of Dadaist picture called the Merz collage. (The word *Merz* was taken from part of the name of a German bank.) His works included trash, such as discarded train tickets, newspapers, and bus transfers. He selected the items of trash for their color and texture as well as their shock value. Schwitters even built a Merz house! It was destroyed in World War II, but it looked like a strange cave with wooden squares and triangles nailed to the inside.

ABOUT THE MEDIA

This artist used bits of discarded trash such as wire, string, rags, newspaper, and tickets in his pictures. He nailed or glued these things onto board or paper.

ABOUT THE TECHNIQUE

Schwitters collected things that people threw away and junk lying on the street. He took these things and put them into his artwork. Schwitters carefully considered the elements of color and texture as he selected the materials. He cut them up so that they fit together and then glued them to paper or wood.

About the Artist

Snowden was born in Detroit, Michigan. She decided at a very young age to become an artist. She attended art school at Wayne State University in Detroit. Early in her career, she made art that celebrated her life and the people around her. In 1987, both of Snowden's parents died. This tragedy changed the direction of her artwork. Her art gained more depth and purpose. Snowden still lives in Detroit. She teaches there as an associate professor at the Center for Creative Studies College of Art and Design.

ABOUT THE ART HISTORY

Snowden uses abstract expressionist techniques. She follows her impulses in applying color to her canvases. Instead of controlling her hands as she paints and draws, she lets them move freely. This technique results in unpredictable, abstract artworks. Snowden chooses to use this technique because she feels that the world is unpredictable. She believes she can express this unpredictability through her art.

Courtesy of Gilda Snowden

ABOUT THE ARTWORK

Snowden groups her artwork into three categories: Tributes, Tornadoes, and Self-Portraits. Tributes are sculptures dedicated to her family and friends. They reflect her memories or feelings for these people. Tornadoes are paintings that express whirlwind energy. Self-Portraits are similar to the Tornadoes in style, but the forms on the canvases vaguely resemble a head and shoulders.

ABOUT THE MEDIA

Snowden creates her Tributes out of plywood and a variety of found objects, including photographs. To these, she applies wax and paint. Her two-dimensional art is made of charcoal and pastel on paper and oil paint on canvas.

ABOUT THE TECHNIQUE

Snowden creates her Tributes by building up layer after layer of objects, wax, and paint onto a plywood base. Sometimes she includes mysterious letters and symbols. In her Tornadoes and Self-Portraits, Snowden uses sharp strokes of color moving in different directions. She likes to apply black, reds, purples, and blues to a solid background color.

Frank Stella (frangk stel´ ə)
(1936–   )

About the Artist

Frank Stella was born in Malden, Massachusetts, in 1936. He studied painting at Phillips Academy and majored in history at Princeton University. He supported himself after college by painting houses. He moved to New York where he had his first successful show called Sixteen Americans. He was 23 years old, the youngest artist in the show. At first, people were annoyed and shocked by his style. However, his talent was noticed by a few important gallery owners and critics who felt his work was exciting and new. Later in his life, he also became an architect.

ABOUT ART HISTORY

Stella began to paint at the end of the influences of abstract expressionism. He was not an emotional painter like Jackson Pollock. Stella wanted to paint essential art. This meant reducing painting to strict geometric designs. He belonged to a group of artists called the "Hard-edge" painters. This group used geometric shapes and little color in their work.

ABOUT THE ARTWORK

Stella's first exhibited works were black, pinstripe paintings. This style paved the way for minimalism. In the 1960s, he experimented with bright colors and odd-shaped canvasses. He produced many series of paintings. One of the best known of these is the protractor series that was made of large circles, half circles, and bright colors. In the late 1970s, he combined an earlier

Thomas Hoepker/Magnum Photos

expressionistic style with three-dimensional canvasses that project nearly two feet into the viewer's face. They are still considered paintings because they must be viewed from the front.

ABOUT THE MEDIA

Stella uses oil paint, sometimes in metallic finishes. In building huge painted canvases, he uses wood to prop up his paintings.

ABOUT THE TECHNIQUE

Stella's work is painted freehand. He begins by drawing guidelines on the canvas. He then fills in the space between the lines with paint. He leaves the white canvas showing between bands of paint. Sometimes he uses canvases in "U" and "L" shapes.

George Sugarman (jôrj shug´ ər mən)
(1912–   )

About the Artist

George Sugarman was born in New York City in 1912. He began to paint in 1950. The following year, he went to Paris, France, on the G.I. Bill program and studied sculpture with the Russian-born sculptor, Ossip Zadkine. He was inspired to develop his own unique style of wood sculpture. He returned to New York and had his first exhibition in 1960. By 1969, he was one of the most celebrated sculptors in the United States. He has had many one-man shows and has won many awards and grants for his artwork.

ABOUT ART HISTORY

George Sugarman was one of the first sculptors to consider the negative space around his sculptures as part of the sculpture itself. Because of this, he thinks about gallery and museum spaces while creating his artwork. In the 1960s, critics thought this technique was experimental and daring. Today many artists, including sculptors, painters, and performance artists, consider gallery spaces as they create their art.

ABOUT THE ARTWORK

Sugarman creates enormous, sprawling forms of laminated wood. His sculptures have unexpected curves and zigzags. They reach out into the spaces around them. Sugarman uses his sculptures to explore his ideas about space. He is interested in filling up gallery and

Courtesy George Sugarman

public spaces in unique ways. One technique he uses is to create sequences of small forms that wander over the length of a gallery and still seem like one unified piece.

ABOUT THE MEDIA

Sugarman creates his sculptures out of wood. Some of his artwork is covered with polychrome, a water-resistant, glossy paint.

ABOUT THE TECHNIQUE

Sugarman works in an expressionist manner when planning his sculptures. The shapes are playful, improvised, and often unexpected. Critics find some of his sculptures remarkable because they are set in such a way that they look like they do not touch the floor for support. Sugarman is a master at bending wood into the shapes he desires.

Agnes Tait (ag´ nəs tāt)
(1897–1981)

About the Artist

Agnes Tait was born in New York City in 1897. Her art training was at the National Academy of Design. Until the Depression, which began with the stock market crash of 1929, Tait was able to show her work regularly. However, with a poor economy, people did not buy art. Through the Work Projects Administration, thousands of people, including artists, were given jobs. Tait was able to go on painting. In 1943, funding by the WPA ended. Tait moved to Santa Fe, New Mexico, to live in an artists' colony. Later, she became well known for her illustrations in children's books.

The Denver Public Library,
Western History Department

ABOUT ART HISTORY

The Work Projects Administration was created to put unemployed people to work. It provided government jobs so that people could continue to support themselves. It had almost nine million workers before it ended in 1943. Among the workers were artists like Tait. Other painters, sculptors, and printmakers also found work. They produced work on and inside government buildings across the United States. Close to 10,000 paintings, sculptures, and drawings were produced through the WPA.

ABOUT THE ARTWORK

Before the Depression, Tait painted pictures of flower still lifes and animals. During the Depression, her work changed to depict people and places. Supported by the federal government's Work Projects Administration, she followed their guidelines to make pictures that reflected the positive aspects of American life.

ABOUT THE MEDIA

Tait used oil on large canvasses, usually over several feet in height and width.

ABOUT THE TECHNIQUE

Tait's paintings express moods and emotions. To convey the cold, she used hues of blue. To tell the time of day, she deepened the color of the sky. Her style is simple and straightforward yet quite detailed.

31

About the Artist

Torres-García was born in Uruguay. His family moved to Spain when he was 17 years old. An eager student and deep thinker, he studied many subjects, including art. As a young man, Torres-García illustrated magazines, created murals, and taught art classes to support himself. He became friends with Pablo Picasso and other young Spanish artists. He married one of his students in 1909. In 1915, Torres-García designed wooden toys with interchangeable parts to amuse his three children. He moved to New York, where he hoped to sell the toys. However, they were too difficult to reproduce. After trying to sell his toys in Italy, Torres-García and his family settled in Paris. He began to use abstract primitive figures in his paintings and sold many of them. He then moved back to Uruguay and opened a successful art school. He also wrote and published articles and books, including an autobiography.

ABOUT ART HISTORY

Torres-García helped found Cercle et Carré (Circle and Square), a group of abstract artists in Paris. The group held exhibitions together and published reviews of abstract art. In his own work, Torres-García combined elements of ancient pre-Columbian art of South America with elements of modern European art.

ABOUT THE ARTWORK

Early in his career, this artist painted realistic landscapes and murals. In time, Torres-García's work became more abstract and was organized by vertical and horizontal lines. Torres-García filled his

Cecilia De Torres, Ltd.

work with signs and symbols representing people, places, and ideas. He even invented his own alphabet and used it in some of his paintings.

ABOUT THE MEDIA

Torres-García worked in oils, watercolors, and ink. He also created murals, wooden sculptural pieces, and toys.

ABOUT THE TECHNIQUE

Torres-García was fascinated with structure. He used lines and color to organize his paintings. Sometimes he drew grids over his paintings to divide them into sections.

Harold Town (hâr´ əld toun)
(1924 – 1990)

About the Artist

Town was born in Toronto, Canada, and painted in that city for almost all of his life. He exhibited his work with a group of Canadian painters called the Painters Seven. He had his first one-person show when he was 30 years old. He created paintings and drawings in many styles.

ABOUT ART HISTORY

Town is usually called an *eclectic* artist because he painted in so many styles. Some of the ideas for his paintings came from the art of Native Americans and Vikings. Other works used images from Japanese or Chinese paintings.

ABOUT THE ARTWORK

Some of Town's paintings look like big, colorful cartoons of muscle men. He also drew pictures of people with oddly shaped bodies. Other works are entirely abstract. He sometimes painted detailed and colorful patterns that make people want to touch his paintings.

T. Bock/Toronto Star Syndicate

ABOUT THE MEDIA

This artist generally worked with oil paints on pressed wooden board or canvas. Town also made collages, black-and-white prints, and ink drawings.

ABOUT THE TECHNIQUE

Many of Town's paintings have decorative designs. He drew such simple shapes as squares or triangles all over a canvas and painted them with vivid colors, such as bright blue or hot pink. In his collages, he glued on colored pieces of paper and painted them, too. In his series of muscle men paintings, he drew the men's huge arms and legs with bold strokes of paint.

Vincent van Gogh (vin sent´ van gō´)
(1853 – 1890)

About the Artist

Even as a boy in Holland, van Gogh cared about other people very much. He tried many jobs, including being a teacher, minister, and social worker. However, he had problems getting along with nearly everyone except his younger brother, Theo. At the age of 28, van Gogh decided that the best way he could serve others was through art. He expressed his deep feelings about people through his paintings. As he moved from place to place, he left many of his works behind. Some were burned in fireplaces for heat or even used to patch holes in walls. Van Gogh was quite poor his entire life and often went hungry so that he could buy painting supplies. Van Gogh died at age 37.

ABOUT ART HISTORY

Even though van Gogh sold only one painting in his lifetime, today he is considered the greatest nineteenth century Dutch artist. He was one of the first to express his feelings through painting. This new school of art is now called Expressionism.

ABOUT THE ARTWORK

Van Gogh painted many different subjects, from portraits to landscapes. He once lived in France near fields of golden wheat and sunflowers, which he painted many times. He wrote that his sunflowers symbolized his gratitude toward others, especially his brother, one of the few people who encouraged him to paint.

Self Portrait with Straw Hat

ABOUT THE MEDIA

During the ten short years that van Gogh worked, he created hundreds of oil paintings, along with many drawings in ink, crayon, chalk, and charcoal.

ABOUT THE TECHNIQUE

Van Gogh wanted to show energy and motion in his work. He often put complementary colors, such as red and green, next to each other to add power to his paintings. He applied oil paints in thick layers, sometimes straight from the tubes. His thick layers, slashing brush strokes, and swirling shapes gave his paintings strong patterns that reflected his strong feelings.

Jan Vermeer (yän vər mir´)
(1632 – 1675)

About the Artist

Jan Vermeer was a Dutch painter born in Delft in 1632. Although little is known about his life, we know that he married at the age of 21 and was the father of 11 children. Vermeer served a six-year apprenticeship and was admitted to the Delft painters guild in 1653. He made a modest living as an art dealer running a business that was left to him by his father. There are no records to show that he sold any of his own works. In 1675, he died in Delft at the age of 45.

Forgotten for almost 200 years, Vermeer is now regarded as one of the greatest painters of all time. This is remarkable because only 35 of his paintings are known to exist. The small number of works are attributed to his deliberate, methodical work habits, his short life, and the disappearance of many of his paintings during the period of obscurity following his death.

ABOUT ART HISTORY
Like other Dutch artists of the seventeenth century, Vermeer painted genre scenes, landscapes, and portraits for the wealthy, middle, business class of the Netherlands. This was different from the artwork produced in Southern Europe at the time, which was primarily religious.

ABOUT THE ARTWORK
Dutch genre painting reached its peak with Vermeer's work. He was a master of stillness. He could capture a moment of life with all action seeming to cease. The subject matter in his work is not as important as his depiction of light and space. He usually used his wife and children as models.

Erich Lessing/Art Resource, NY

ABOUT THE MEDIA
Vermeer painted with oil paint on canvas or wood grounds.

ABOUT THE TECHNIQUE
Vermeer was a master of optical reality. He included only the details that you would see from a normal distance. His use of color and value were also consistent with what you would actually see. He painted slowly and painstakingly, completing two or three works a year. The textures of objects are so realistic that the viewer is tempted to touch the surface to see how it feels.

Patricia Walker (pə trish´ə wôl´ kər)
(1949–   )

About the Artist

Patricia Walker was born in Natrona Heights, Pennsylvania, located near the Allegheny River. She received her degree in painting from the Rhode Island School of Design in 1985. In 1987, she completed her Master of Fine Arts degree in painting from Cornell University. Since the fall of 1987, she has enjoyed teaching fine arts at Georgia Southern University.

Courtesy of Patricia Walker

ABOUT ART HISTORY

Walker has been influenced by many artists including Matisse, De Kooning, and Giotti. What intrigues her about these artists is the way they break down flat spaces with abstracted grounds, figures, and objects.

ABOUT THE ARTWORK

Patricia Walker paints many still lifes with objects and parts of figures in abstracted spaces. The use of abstraction in her work reflects an emotional and psychological place that is further enhanced by her choice of colors. This painting is part of a still-life series that includes 20 pieces. Many of these paintings include fragmented images of body parts. Much of her new work deals with the whole human figure.

ABOUT THE MEDIA

Walker works in pastels, charcoal, or gouache. She frequently makes pencil drawings that are as large as 5×4 feet. She paints in oil on canvas or on rag paper.

ABOUT THE TECHNIQUE

Walker often starts her work with images in mind, usually an abstract composition. She slowly starts to develop elements of shapes and patterns into images. She feels that painting is like a jigsaw puzzle that has many shapes that one must play around with until they fit together.

Antoine Watteau (än twän wä tō)
(1684–1721)

About the Artist

Watteau is regarded as one of the outstanding artists of the Rococo period, and a forerunner of French Impressionsim. In Paris, he studied under the engraver and stage designer Claude Gillot, painting scenes of the comedy groups that performed at French fairs. Next, Watteau painted scenes that were part of the interior decoration of mansions. He competed twice for the Prix de Rome. The prize would have paid his way to Rome to study art. He did not win the prize, but he got the judges' attention with his unusual subject matter—social gatherings of elegant people in park settings. In time, Watteau's paintings became very popular, and he was admitted to France's Royal Academy of Art. He died at age 37.

ABOUT ART HISTORY

Watteau invented the fête galante. In this type of painting, well-dressed people talk or play musical instruments in a parklike setting. Watteau was deeply influenced by the painting style of Peter Paul Rubens.

ABOUT THE ARTWORK

In Watteau's graceful version of a fête galante, people show their affection for each other subtly, with meaningful glances. Some are dressed in ordinary clothing, while others wear costumes, like actors in a play.

Giraudon/Art Resource, NY

ABOUT THE MEDIA

Watteau painted in oils and drew in pencil and colored chalk, especially red, white, and black. At times, he used pastels and watercolors.

ABOUT THE TECHNIQUE

Watteau created scenes by selecting figures from sketches he made in a notebook. He placed these figures in a setting that he liked.

Mola (Kuna)   (mohl ah)   (koon ah)

About the Artist

The Kuna Indians live on the islands of the San Blas Archipelago off of the eastern coast of Panama. In the sixteenth century, they were an important culture and lived in central Panama. But European contact ruined the Kuna's society by destroying their religious and social customs. Now, the 40,000 remaining Kuna live in small villages. Most families earn a living by farming or fishing. Some people are forced to go to Panama City to make money.

ABOUT THE ART HISTORY

Molas are only one form of Kuna art. Recently, drawing has become a very important part of Kuna history and life. Although the Kuna Indians like their primitive lifestyles and are trying to resist change, the Kuna culture is quickly becoming more modernized. They want to preserve their past, but they have no written language except for sacred hieroglyphs. So they are capturing their culture by making picture stories. These pictures are being collected in archives so Kuna Indians of the future will know how the Kuna lived in the past.

ABOUT THE ARTWORK

Mola is the Kuna word for cloth. Mola blouses are decorated with decorative panels on the front and the back. The complex, bright designs reflect Kuna beliefs, daily activities, and the environment around them.

Kuna Women. *(Panama).* Mola: Group Project of Kuna Women. *Layered and cut fabric with stitchery. Private Collection. Photograph by © Frank Fortune.*

They show plants, birds, animals, and themes from Kuna mythology and the Bible. The patterns are abstract and based on the general shapes the Kuna find in the coral in the ocean around them.

ABOUT THE MEDIA

The Kuna make their mola blouses out of cloth bought in Panama City or island shops. They also use needles, thread, and scissors to make the molas.

ABOUT THE TECHNIQUE

Mola appliqué requires a cloth base and a covering layer of a contrasting color. The top layer is partially cut away to reveal shapes and color underneath. Additional layers of sections of cloth may be inserted beneath the top layer. Small patches of cloth may be sewn on the top layer. Sewing is done by hand and machine. Lines of chain-stitching, a type of embroidery, is used to decorate uncut areas of cloth.

Man's Headband of Toucan Feathers

About the Artist

This headband was made by an unidentified Shuar or Achuar peoples from Ecuador. Ecuador is part of the Amazon basin. The Amazon covers an area of about six million square miles and extends into nine countries—Peru, Brazil, Ecuador, Colombia, Bolivia, Venezuela, French Guyana, Guyana, and Surinam. Five hundred different tribes live in the Amazon. Each tribe has its own language, beliefs, and customs. All believe that they share the forest with the animals and the plants. When Europeans arrived in South America, as many as 12 to 15 million Indians lived in the Amazon. Since then, millions have died from Western diseases or cruel treatment. Amazonian tribes are still struggling to keep their lands and culture.

ABOUT ART HISTORY

The Shuar live in the eastern lowlands of Ecuador. They created an organization known as the *Federacion Interprovincial de Centro Shuar-Achuar.* Part of the group's mission is to be sure that museum collections represent these tribes as a living, vital culture in the Amazon region. Because both tribes still exist, they do not want museums acting as if they are extinct.

Artist unknown. (Ecuador). Man's Headband of Toucan Feathers. *Courtesy of the National Museum of the American Indian, New York, New York. Photo by David Heald.*

This headband is a woven cotton band decorated with red and yellow toucan feathers and black feathers from a bird called the awacha. The headband has danglers that look like earrings. These are made from toucan feathers and human hair.

ABOUT THE MEDIA

The headbands are made of cotton, feathers, human hair, and thread. Tools needed to create a headband include a loom and a needle.

ABOUT THE ARTWORK

Feathered headbands are worn by older men and political leaders in the Shuar and Achuar tribes as symbols of bravery and authority. Usually headbands are worn only during celebrations and other special occasions.

ABOUT THE TECHNIQUE

First, the cotton band is woven on a loom. Then, feathers and human hair are sewn on for decoration. Hair is taken only from living people who volunteer to cut their hair as a contribution to the headband.

The Giant Stone Moai

About the Artist

Easter Island is about 2,300 miles west of Chile in the South Pacific Ocean. Its earliest settlers created the statues that made the island famous. Scientists think that Easter Island was settled about A.D. 400, but they are not sure who the first settlers were. Some think they were Native Americans, others say they were Polynesians. Many of the islanders were killed during a war between two of the groups around 1860. Others were captured in Peruvian slave raids. When a few of them were returned, they brought diseases and more islanders died. In 1877, only 110 people remained there. Since then, the native population has grown, and Chileans have moved to Easter Island.

ABOUT ART HISTORY

Archaeologists think that the statues on Easter Island may represent important people who lived there. The statues may have been created so that islanders could worship people after they died. Through time, many of the statues were knocked over. Some lost their hatlike cylinders or their eyes. The Chilean government has made Easter Island a national park to help preserve its culture and landscape. The government has restored some of the huge stone figures, including replacing the coral and stone eyes and the red topknots.

ABOUT THE ARTWORK

More than 600 statues are scattered around Easter Island. They were originally arranged in rows of up to a dozen statues. Most of the statues are from 10 to 20 feet tall. Some are as high as 40 feet and weigh up to 90 tons. Their eye cavities are deep and oval and

Artist unknown. (Polynesia). The Giant Stone Moai. *c. A.D. 1000–1500, restored 1978. Ahu Nau Nau, Easter Island, Polynesia. Volcanic stone (tufa), average height approximately 36 feet. © George Halton/Photo Researchers, Inc.*

contain coral and stone eyes. The angular faces of the statues are carved on the same stone as their solid bodies. Huge, red cylindrical crowns were balanced on the heads of some of the statues.

ABOUT THE MEDIA

The statues were carved out of volcanic rock with stone hand-picks. It is thought that the rock was moved with levers made of wooden logs.

ABOUT THE TECHNIQUE

The islanders used stone hand picks to carve the statues from the rock of an extinct volcano. Each statue had its front and sides completed to a polish before the back was detached from the volcano. The statue was then slid away and raised. Once the monument had been erected in its final resting spot, the eyes and red topknots were added.

Stonehenge

About the Artist

Stonehenge is a prehistoric ritual monument that is set on the Salisbury Plain, north of Salisbury, England. The people who built Stonehenge had widespread European trade connections. They settled in the area between 1600 and 1300 B.C. In 1964, an American astronomer, Gerald S. Hawkins, used a computer to coordinate the measurements of Stonehenge with astronomical information from about 1500 B.C. He concluded that this monument could have been used to predict vernal and autumnal equinoxes, as well as eclipses of the sun and moon. He also suggested that it was used as a daily calendar.

ABOUT ART HISTORY

Stonehenge is the most complex of the 40 to 50 prehistoric circular megalith monuments in the British Isles. Natural forces or human activity have caused standing stones to fall over and ditches to fill with dirt. Some people probably took stones away to make bridges or dams. R. J. C. Atkinson, a British archaeologist, began making excavations at Stonehenge in the 1950s. Stonehenge is now a major tourist spot, attracting more than one million visitors a year.

Stonehenge. © 1984 Lawrence Migdale/Photo Researchers Inc.

ABOUT THE ARTWORK

The monument is made of concentric rings of stone. The outermost ring is 100 feet in diameter and made of large, sandstone blocks called sarsen stones. These sarsen stones are placed upright with lintels on top. Inside the outermost ring is a circle of smaller bluestones spotted with dolorite. Within that circle is a horseshoe-shaped set of bluestones enclosing a mica-type stone slab. This stone slab is called the Altar Stone. Near the entrance lies a sarsen stone known as the Slaughter Stone.

ABOUT THE MEDIA

Gray sandstone and bluestones were used to build Stonehenge. The builders probably used ropes, pulleys, and logs to transport the stones. Some sort of primitive tool was used to curve and taper the rocks.

ABOUT THE TECHNIQUE

Stonehenge was built in three phases from 2800 to 1500 B.C. Some of the rocks used to build Stonehenge were moved from more than 150 miles away. The visible surfaces of the rocks were smoothed. Then, the rocks were carefully shaped to form projections and holes so that the stones would lock together. Researchers estimate that it took about 30 million man-hours over hundreds of years to build Stonehenge.

Corn Palace

About the Artist

A variety of architects, contractors, and artists have worked on the Corn Palace in South Dakota. The current building was designed by architects Rapp and Rapp of Chicago. This architectural firm also designed Radio City Music Hall in New York City and many other famous theatrical buildings in the United States. The exterior designs, which are changed every year, are created by different people from year to year. Five of the interior panels were designed by world-famous artist, Oscar Howe.

ABOUT ART HISTORY

The first Corn Palace was built in 1892 to celebrate the fertile farmland in Mitchell, South Dakota, and to promote settlement of the area. The success of the Corn Belt Exposition, held inside the Palace, prompted building new, larger structures in 1905, 1921, and 1937. In 1937, the Byzantine-inspired minarets, turrets, and kiosks were added. During the winter months of 1919-1920, the dirt floor was flooded, and the Corn Palace served as South Dakota's first indoor skating rink! In 1979, the Palace caught fire but was saved by local firefighters. In 1987, the building received renovations costing $650,000.

ABOUT THE ARTWORK

The Corn Palace is covered from top to bottom with native grasses, grains, and a variety of colored corn. These are arranged in attractive designs. Because of the effects of

Artist Unknown. Corn Palace. *Mitchell, South Dakota.*
© *Peter Pearson/Tony Stone Worldwide.*

weather and hungry birds, the exterior must be changed every year. One of the permanent interior panels shows pheasant hunting, a popular pastime in the area.

ABOUT THE MEDIA

The Corn Palace is covered with thousands of bushels of dock, wild oats, brome grass, bluegrass, rye straw, and wheat, along with other grains and corn.

ABOUT THE TECHNIQUE

By September of every year, the decorations are removed, and a new decor is applied. Workers stand on tubular steel scaffolding and use air nailers and staplers to put up the grains, corn, and grasses. Wheat and straw are first tied in bunches. Corn is cut to the required lengths with a specially designed table saw. The total annual cost of decorating can vary from $25,000 to $60,000, depending on the amount of surface to be worked.

Lacquer Box

About the Artist

Lacquer boxes are handmade by individual artists. After the Russian Revolution, artists who had been trained to make religious icons began painting genre and folktale scenes on lacquer boxes.

ABOUT ART HISTORY

Lacquered objects of wood or metal coated with a resinous varnish were brought to Europe from China and Persia in the sixteenth century. The first known use of lacquer in Russia was in Peter the Great's palace, which was built around 1720. Inside was a room decorated with 94 lacquered panels painted by Russian artists. In the second half of the eighteenth century, lacquered objects became popular. Russian artists made many small lacquered objects such as snuffboxes and medals. In the nineteenth century, entire villages of artists devoted themselves to producing lacquered objects.

ABOUT THE ARTWORK

The boxes show a variety of genre scenes and illustrations of Russian folktales and legends, such as *The Firebird* and *The Frog Prince*.

Artist Unknown. *(Russian).* Lacquer Box. *1991. Wood with oil paint and lacquer. Hudak private collection.*

Some artists specialize in making boxes with Chinese designs or floral designs.

ABOUT THE MEDIA

The boxes are made of cardboard or paper, glue, lacquer, and paint. An oven, a wooden block, and a wooden frame are all necessary tools for making a lacquered box.

ABOUT THE TECHNIQUE

The process of making lacquered boxes takes about 70 days. Strips of cardboard or paper are glued together and wound around a wooden block. They are then placed inside a wooden frame. The frame is pressed inward to form a box as hard as wood. Workers coat the box with layers of lacquer, drying it in an oven after each coat. Then, an artist paints a design on the lid and around the sides. Finally, the box is given several coats of clear lacquer, dried, and polished by hand.

About the Artist

This plaque of hammered gold was found in a burial site near the head of an important local chief. The plaque was made in Cocle, a province of central Panama on that nation's southern coast. It was made sometime between A.D. 700 and 1100. The artist is unknown.

ABOUT ART HISTORY

Art objects made by the indigenous people of Cocle were discovered on and off from about 1850. In 1915, archaeologists figured out that one local culture had created the art. Formal excavations began in 1925. From 1930 to 1933, extensive work was done in Cocle. Archaeologists found artifacts made of gold, copper, and other metals. Some items were carved out of bone or ivory. They also found textiles and pottery. All of the artifacts were found in burial sites. The plaque shown here is from a 1931 archaeological dig conducted by Harvard University. The excavation was funded by the Brooklyn Museum.

ABOUT THE ARTWORK

This plaque shows a pattern of a creature

Artist unknown. Plaque. *700–1100 A.D. Gold. 22.9 × 21.6 cm. The Brooklyn Museum, New York, New York. Peabody Museum Expedition to Cocle Province, Panama.*

that seems half human and half reptile. It has big eyes, sharp teeth, and claws on its hands and feet. Crests shoot up out of its head. Patterns commonly found in the Cocle artifacts resemble human heads and bodies, fish, frogs, birds, and monkeys. Some patterns are completely abstract.

ABOUT THE MEDIA

The artist used gold and hammering tools to make the plaque.

ABOUT THE TECHNIQUE

The goldsmith hammered the metal to a thin sheet. Then, designs were embossed on it with a hammering tool. The artist must have worked over a soft surface such as leather or sand in order to make the designs stick up out of the surface of the metal.

Kente Cloth

About the Artist

Kente cloths are made by the Western African Ashanti people of Ghana and the Ewe of Ghana and Togo. The weavers who make kente cloth are always male. The art of weaving kente is passed down from generation to generation.

Artist unknown. Ashanti people (Ghana). Kente cloth. From the Girard Foundation Collection in the Museum of International Folk Art, a unit of the Museum of New Mexico, Santa Fe, New Mexico. Photographer: Michel Monteaux.

ABOUT ART HISTORY

Kente cloth has been worn by African royalty for hundreds of years to show a person's power and prestige. The word *kente* means "that which will not tear away under any condition." Traditional kente cloth is the national costume for the people of Ghana. It is worn for ceremonial occasions, such as festivals, weddings, and births.

In traditional African societies, every piece of art must have a purpose and fulfill a need. Baskets, ceramic storage containers, musical instruments, utensils, furniture, religious icons, buildings, and articles of clothing are all enhanced by African artists.

ABOUT THE ARTWORK

Kente cloth is dazzling and colorful. Bright, primary colors such as red, yellow, and green are woven together into a pattern of lines. Each patchwork pattern is produced by the placement of colors. Each color combination has a different meaning. Red and yellow suggest life and its power over sickness; green and white, a bountiful harvest; and blue, love and the rule of the queen. Men in Ghana drape kente cloth over themselves, and women wear kente skirts.

ABOUT THE MEDIA

Kente cloth is made of silk or cotton fiber. A narrow floor loom is used to hand weave the cloth.

ABOUT THE TECHNIQUE

Kente cloth is woven on narrow looms with floor pedals. The strips are cut into pieces and sewn together side by side.

Chinese Children's Slippers

About the Artist

These slippers were created by an elderly grandmother who sold them on a tiny side street in Shanghai, China.

ABOUT ART HISTORY

Some of the most delightful pieces of Chinese folk art are textiles, including embroideries of cotton and silk. Embroidery, the stitched decoration on clothing and other textiles, has traditionally been one of the few ways a peasant woman could express her sense of beauty and display her artistic skills.

Artist unknown. (China). Chinese Children's Slippers. *1991. Cotton appliqued with silk. 4 × 2 × 1½ inches. Hudak Private Collection. Photograph by © Tom Amedis.*

These enchanting embroideries were most often made to keep children from tripping as they first learned to walk. The embroidered clothes made for little boys play a role in protecting them from evil spirits. When a child is one month old, his or her mother or grandmother may make a tiger hat, tiger pillow, tiger collar, and tiger shoes, which are viewed as both shields and decoration. Tigers are the chosen motif because they are believed to not bother human beings but are ferocious enough to frighten away bad spirits. The child wears the tiger clothing and sleeps on the pillow on his birthdays and during other festivities, such as New Year's.

Unfortunately, China is still a male-dominated society. Sons represent the future of a family. They are given the responsibility for their elders and ancestral spirits. A woman says that her son is her greatest treasure. Giving birth to sons is a status symbol for women. So, the embroideries created especially for her sons receive a woman's deepest attention and love.

Women from traditional China were judged not by their beauty, but by their embroidery skills. Embroidery is one of the oldest forms of artistic and decorative effort in China.

ABOUT THE MEDIA

The slippers are made of cotton, and the designs are embroidered with silk thread.

ABOUT THE ARTWORK

The little tiger faces seen on the front of these shoes were made to help scare away bad spirits and to watch over a child's steps.

ABOUT THE TECHNIQUE

A tiger's face design is first sketched onto the slippers. Then, a woman stitches the pattern into the cotton with silk thread.